OLD NORTH CORNWALL

Hilda Hambly

BOSSINEY BOOKS

First published in 1991 by Bossiney Books,
St Teath, Bodmin, Cornwall.

Typeset and printed by
Penwell Print Ltd, Callington, Cornwall.

ISBN 0 948158 73 5

ACKNOWLEDGEMENTS

FRONT COVER designed and tinted by MAGGIE GINGER

Back cover: The St Breock quartet singing at Lanhydrock in 1905

INTRODUCING OLD NORTH CORNWALL and HILDA HAMBLY

OLD NORTH Cornwall – those three words and the pictures plus text inside these pages, turn the calendar back in quite incredible fashion.

Old photographs and picture postcards generate a fascination for most of us. They are not only evocative, they reflect a mood and way of life that has gone – and gone forever.

Time was when North Cornwall was known as the forgotten land – a time when a number of these photographs were just about to spring from the camera.

Today North Cornwall is no forgotten land. The growth of tourism changed all that. If our grandparents – and their parents – came back, they would, of course, see enormous changes. People from England may make holiday homes here. Modern, and sometimes ugly developments, have sprung up on the fringes of towns and villages. Pylons may march across our lovely varied landscapes. Yet curiously, in many parts, the essential spirit of North Cornwall remains: on brooding Bodmin Moor, along the beautiful but wicked coastline, in some of the secret valleys and along rivers like the Camel and Allen.

North Cornwall is different things to different people: a region defying neat easy classification. In a land so saturated in vivid legend and genuine history, how could it be otherwise?

HILDA HAMBLY was born in 1910 in the lovely village of Trevia near Camelford: the eldest of six children of Mr & Mrs Baker. Her father John worked at the Stannon Clayworks on the edge of Bodmin Moor: 'walking 4 miles there and 4 miles back for a pittance really.

'I started school at the age of four and a half,' she recalls, 'when Camelford School was on the Clease. Soon after starting school I had an accident crushing my finger, swinging on a gate, and I had to have an operation, performed on the dining room table of Dr Jerome, our local Camelford doctor. When I was well enough to return to school, it had moved . . . to the Primary School where it is today.

'Somewhere between the age of five and six years, I remember being terrified at my first sight of a steamroller. I screamed and would not pass it, but a kind gentleman took my hand and guided me around. I later discovered that he was my mother's

▶ *THE AUTHOR outside her home in Eddystone Terrace, Wadebridge enjoying a look at some of her favourite old photographs.*

EDDYSTONE
TERRACE

▲ *HILDA HAMBLY, photographed at Camelford School in 1923. The author is the girl with a white ribbon in her hair, second from the left in the second row from the back. She was then 13 years old.*

► *HENNON BRIDGE, the River Alan, near Camelford. The serviceman enjoys the tranquil scene – almost certainly he is on leave during the years of the Second World War.*

uncle Mr John Best of St Breward who was a local preacher.

'Every morning before school I had to fetch the milk for my mother and a neighbour from Mutly Farm, and I often ran errands into Camelford for our neighbours in Trevia.

'When the Delabole Co-op opened I used to take a short cut across the slate quarry every Saturday to get the shopping. I had to take care to bring home the ticket so that my Dad could calculate how much dividend was due to be collected at Christmas. It was 2s 6d in the pound at one time (12½ p) and that was quite a lot of money in those days. We collected all the water from the pump in our village and on the occasions that it ran dry we had to carry the water all the way from the well at Trevia Walls. Walking to school we had to pass the workhouse at Sportsmans and we were never afraid of the tramps if we met them. For a night's lodge they had to break stones, they often called at our door for a billycan of boiling water to make their tea.

'I left home to live and work in Wadebridge when I was fourteen years but used to travel by train to Camelford to visit my family. Sometimes my mother would walk part of the long dark and lonely road to Camelford Station, but I was never afraid to walk alone. I couldn't do it today.

'When I was married my brothers and sisters used to cycle down through the valley to visit me.

'My first husband Bert Allen was a foundry worker at Oatey and Martins, as was his father before him. He later became a storeman for Tremain and Collicotts, the grocers in Molesworth

Street, which is where Bricknells now have a shop. We had two children, Roy who sadly died aged 2 years, and Margaret who lives and works in Wadebridge, and her son Shaun is my only grandson.

'As Bert was one of a big family we had many happy times together. As there were not trains on a Sunday all the family would walk down the railway line to Roskear along what is now called the Camel Trail. When the tide was out, the middle of the river bed was sandy and the children would play, but we had to keep an eye on the tide. We would watch for the first wave and immediately call the children in. On the long walk home we picked wild strawberries and blackberries.

'The family were all very good singers and the carols at Christmas were most enjoyable. One of Bert's sisters was very superstitious and would make sure there were never thirteen at the table for meals. When mother died, Christmas never seemed the same.

'During the war when the armoured train was in Wadebridge we had a Polish Army lieutenant and his wife to stay with us for a few months. We also had a land army girl and several evacuees. In later years we had several people lodge with us; many have kept in touch and some have become great friends. Our first evacuee, Dick, came back to visit us after many years and later married Margaret Rose who had made her home with us. They have one daughter and live at Bere Alston.

'Most of my first marriage was spent at Wellington Place, not the big estate that it is today, just eighteen houses. We had a corn field in front of us with a wonderful view. The community spirit was amazing, particularly through the second world war. My daughter was an only child but she never felt lonely because of the companionship and friendships which still survive today. We were one big happy family.

'It was quite a race on Monday mornings to see who would be the first with the washing on the line. We had to stoke up the fire under the coppers in the "back kitchen" to boil up the whites. The gardens were also a kind of competition for the menfolk and the vegetables grown in those back gardens kept us well fed during hard times. Every year we had a float in Wadebridge Carnival and everyone looked out for the Wellington Place entry.

'We formed a club called the 19 Club which was held in the garage of the bungalow opposite. We had a committee and arranged collections for outings, parties and trips to Plymouth pantomimes. It is said that this kind of community spirit no longer exists.

'Unfortunately Bert developed multiple sclerosis and I nursed him for thirteen years and for the last four years of his life he was a resident at St Teresa's Cheshire Home at Long Rock, near Penzance. He died just before our fortieth wedding anniversary.

'I later met and married Jerry Hambly who was the track

▶ *HILDA HAMBLY with her projector, ready to give one of her popular slide shows.*

chargehand of a gang of men working between Wadebridge, Wenford and Bodmin Road, and inspector of the closed lines. We took advantage of free travel and we had a very happy time visiting many countries. Jerry was very proud to have served thirteen years as a Royal Marine, and we had fifteen wonderful years together until he sadly died of cancer.

'I have always found it very interesting talking to older people about past events, and my late neighbour Mrs Mabel Philp who died a few years ago at the age of 103 was a wonderful source of information. I have always felt a great responsibility for the photographs and postcards which have been loaned to me, and I must thank all the people who have trusted me with these items.

'I would also like to thank particularly Ray Bishop and Miss May Garland who have helped me so much by producing slides from these photographs in order that I could give illustrated talks. To date I have given 200 slide shows for charity and have about 300 slides and 150 photographs in my collection. The interest is such that after almost every show people give me more information and photographs so that my collection continues to grow and grow.

'I am a honorary member of the Wadebridge Camera Club and try never to miss a meeting. I am proud to have won several merit awards and to have photographs published in tourist brochures and guide books. I am also a member of the Old Cornwall Society.'

Hilda Hambly is a natural communicator, with a real sense of fun. You have only to attend one of her slide shows, and, within five minutes, you know you're destined for an entertaining evening. Moreover she positively encourages audience participation – unlike some such gatherings which are basically 'sermon and slides'. I attended one of her shows at the Betty Fisher Centre on the site of the old Wadebridge station, and, every now and then switched my gaze from the slides to the faces of the audience: absolute fascination. One of the audience that evening was a gentleman who, as a boy, had been an evacuee in Wadebridge during the Hitler war. He had heard about Hilda's show on BBC Radio Cornwall, and delayed his return to Brighton by a day for the very purpose of seeing the Hilda Hambly Collection – and he thoroughly enjoyed his trip down Memory Lane. At the same show were two Wadebridge 'boys' – exiles really – Mr 'Bing' Spear from Windlesham, Surrey, and Mr Ken Hodge from North Berwick, Scotland.

The heart of the matter is Hilda has that rare gift: infectious enthusiasm. It would be a very dreary fellow who was bored with a Hilda Hambly show. As her publisher I have had the luck to see the Hilda Hambly collection informally at her home in Wadebridge – either looking through her splendid albums or seeing some of her 'specials' on the screen – and always the same infectious enthusiasm and pleasure in sharing her pictures

WHITE CROSS Choir early in the century. The author believes that all these members of the choir have now died, including the little girl.

THIS PICTURE was taken at the opening of the showground at Wadebridge. Left to right: Mr Mutton, Sir John Molesworth St Aubyn and Lady St Aubyn, Mr Key, Mr Percy Spear, Mr Blackwell, and behind, Mr Button. The Royal Cornwall Show has grown into one of the most important events in the Cornish calendar. Under one name or another, the show has been going strong since 1793. It was granted its Royal Charter way back in 1827, and has been permanently based at Wadebridge since 1960.

and her knowledge.

Hilda's public performance is remarkable on two scores: first, she rattles off dates and names without a single note and secondly she verbally gives us pinsharp snapshots of North Cornwall all those years ago. The slides are good, and newspaper editors have been saying for generations 'A picture is worth a thousand words'. Nevertheless without Hilda's skilful commentary, these shows would lose a great deal.

Her fund of stories is rich. My favourite concerns an unsure young girl who came to do her first day's work at a Wadebridge cafe. 'Go upstairs and get changed,' she was told by the proprietors. 'We expect to be very busy for the next couple of hours.' Over two hours later, somebody went in search of the newcomer. She was still upstairs. 'I didn't come down,' the girl nervously explained, 'because I knew you'd be busy.'

That great American the late Truman Capote would have approved of Hilda Hambly's style. He once reflected: I devoutly believe that the taking of notes – much less the use of a tape recorder! – distorts or even destroys any naturalness that might exist between the observer and the observed.'

Cornwall has drawn creative spirits – painters, potters and sculptors – like a magnet. This book is a reminder how Cornwall, and North Cornwall in particular, has inspired photographers too. There is a timeless quality in many of the photographs in the Hilda Hambly Collection. These artist photographers – and they are just that – have somehow suspended time itself.

Some of the subjects, of course, have a self-conscious air – we must remember they were 'shot' in days long, long before the television screen came into our rooms, they were 'shot' when men with cameras were rare. Some of the photographs though are incredibly natural – so much so that one recalls a sitter for Cecil Beaton saying: 'sitting for Beaton has a sense of slightly

THE RESIDENCE of Mr Edwards, the famous Cornish bone setter, at Sladebridge. People came hundreds of miles to get help from this man with 'healing hands'.

drifting in space – of not being photographed but painted, and painted by a casual, barely visible presence.'

It was in fact a well known present day North Cornwall photographer, Ray Bishop, who recommended Hilda as a Bossiney author. In reality Hilda came to Bossiney on a double recommendation, the other being Chris Day, the Chairman of the North Cornwall National Trust Association. Chris had attended a Hilda Hambly slide show the previous evening, and was so impressed that he felt moved to telephone and suggest her as a possible Bossiney author.

Wadebridge naturally is the window of her world. Standing at the head of the Camel Estuary, the town got its name from the old English word meaning a ford, or possibly the Latin *vadum*.

The bridge is the great Wadebridge landmark and symbol – arguably one of the famous and most photographed in the whole of the Westcountry.

Gone are the sailing ships. Even in our twentieth century they came up here, and you can still see the old wharves and quays. 'When the tide is out,' wrote Arthur Norway, 'it is as though the town has lost its soul.' And we must remember in his day the Camel was less silted with sand and mud.

But Hilda's collection is not the Wadebridge of today with its yellow lines and traffic wardens, not the town of traffic jams and TV aerials, and when she ventures to other places in North Cornwall, she – and this book – take us back in mood and time.

THE CORONATION of King Edward in 1902. The tobacconists' was owned by Mr & Mrs Hawke, and Ella, their daughter. Tobacco was then four pence an ounce. Ella Hawke carried on the business after her parents died. This shop is now a building society office.

A WELLINGTON PLACE entry in the Wadebridge Carnival. The children look rather solemn, perhaps concentrating on keeping their balance on the back of the slowly-moving lorry.

WINTER IN Coronation Park, Wadebridge.

MOLESWORTH STREET is the main Wadebridge thoroughfare. The Molesworth Arms, seen in both pictures, is one of the most interesting buildings in the town – a sixteenth century inn with ghostly claims. Tradition has it that a phantom coach, drawn by four horses and driven by a headless coachman, travels through the courtyard at midnight on New Year's Eve. It was first known as The Fox, later rechristened The King's Arms, and then The Fountain. In 1817 the landlord John Stephens gave the inn its present name out of respect for the family who lived on the other side of the river at Pencarrow. The Molesworths, who once owned the building, were the principal landowners hereabouts, and the family crest is over the main entrance, while in the entrance hall hangs a picture of the Rt Hon Sir William Molesworth, Bart, a former Member of Parliament and Secretary of State for the Colonies.

A PEACEFUL view of Wadebridge and the River Camel.

STYLE
AND
QUALITY
HOTEL

FISHING
TACKLE
BREAD
SIMONDS
GARAGE
HOTEL
MOLESWORTH STREET, WADEBRIDGE

STURDY OXEN pull the cart advertising Atora suet along Molesworth Street. The picture was taken in 1924 and shows Mr Paul's shoe shop, and Lobb's sweet shop. Mr Lobb is standing in the doorway with his daughter. The man wearing the trilby hat is Mr Shearstone who owned the ironmonger's shop further up Molesworth Street.

MEMBERS OF The Ancient Order of Foresters coming down Molesworth Street towards the bridge. John Hawken's Railway Stores is now a shoe shop.

THE fifteenth century bridge at Wadebridge is one of the great landmarks of North Cornwall. By tradition the ford hereabouts was so difficult and dangerous that a chapel was built on both banks of the Camel so travellers could pray for a safe crossing in one chapel and then offer up thanks in the other. It was around 1470 when the vicar of Egloshayle, Thomas Loveybond, started raising money to build the much-needed bridge, but the builders soon ran into difficulties – a matter of finding strong enough foundations for the piers. North Cornwall folklore has it that the problem was solved by building on wool packs. Some say the caring vicar had a vision in which he was shearing sheep brought to him by an angel. The wool falling into the water gave Thomas Loveybond an inspired thought: 'Why not use wool sacks as a foundation?' Others say the money was raised from a tax on wool sales. Either way, the bridge was first completed in 1485. The original bridge was 320 feet long and a mere nine feet wide with seventeen Gothic arches – the architect had angles over each pier as a refuge for the pedestrians from the horse traffic. In 1852-53 the bridge was widened by three feet on either side, and there was a further widening in 1963 when planners and builders showed commendable skill and care in preserving its character. Consequently Wadebridge can boast a 500-year old bridge in constant use.

This verse was inscribed on parchment and placed inside the plaque commemorating the widening of the bridge. Rebuilding took 74 weeks.

In Cornwall, east of Wadebridge town
There is a bridge of great renown
The River Camel at high tide
Laps the banks at either side.
A fair bridge built by Loveybond
A vicar from the town beyond.
Thirteen gothic arches stand
Bedded deep in shifting sand
On sacks of wool they laid the piers
And these have stood five hundred years.

The old bridge with increasing load
Demanded then a wider road.
And so one day contractors came
Called Cleveland Bridge, a famous name.
Lofty cranes on Gabbard High
Towered upwards to the sky.
Piles were driven deep below
And local people watched it grow.
Some shook their heads, expressing doubt
As ancient cracks were filled with grout.

Machines and men worked on the site
Through summer days and in the night.
Shutters, coffer dams and caissons
Scaffolding and stone for masons
Welding plant, cement and sand
Covered the surrounding land.
Lorries came and tipped their load
Drains were laid along the road
Skilled engineers with planned design
Rebuilt the bridge in record time.

POLMORLA MILL with Mrs Mary Roose in the picture. The mill was owned by the Duchy of Cornwall. The Queen Mother and King George VI visited this very beautiful old Cornish building in the 1940s.

A RARE old photograph: cattle in the Camel by the Egloshayle Road with Egloshayle Church in the background.

DO RAILWAY stations still attract children? Times were when children were drawn to stations like magnets – and train spotting was a popular hobby. Here are two youngsters at Wadebridge station, Piran and Wenna Bishop, son and daughter of the well-known Bossiney photographer.

THE SIDEWAYS glances of these Wadebridge schoolboys are probably of apprehension. The photographer, Mr Oatey, lined them up and told them to eat the pasties while he took their picture. The lads had brought the pasties to Cornwall Farmers for their fathers' dinners and after the shutter had clicked had to face their hungry parents and tell them the pasties were gone! The photograph was taken before the First World War and the boys are Archie Rickard, Mervyn Rickard, George Henry Dore and George Beare.

COMFORT, ATTENTION and a good cuisine were promised in the brochure from Molesworth Arms proprietor Capt R.W. Johnson. However, a bath was a shilling extra on the bill ...

TARIFF

APARTMENTS.

Single Room	6/-
Double „	10/6
Double „ two beds	12/-

MEALS.

Breakfast	3/-	Dinner	5/-
Luncheon	3/6	Supper (cold) ... from	3/-
Tea (Plain)	1/6		

EXTRAS.

Bath	1/-	Fire in Bedroom—	
Meals served in Bedroom ...		evening ...	2/-
	6d. per person	day	3/6
Early Morning Tea	6d.	Garage per night ...	1/-

Inclusive Terms by arrangement.

WADEBRIDGE POST Office with customers but no staff in sight. The office was owned by Mr Herbie Ennor from the turn of the century until it was refurbished and the new post office opened.

WHITE CROSS Skittle Group. The second from the left is Mr Hicks, and the fourth from the left is Mr Sloggett from Whitecross.

A PROUD OCCASION for the people of Wadebridge during the Second World War as they present a cheque for two Lancaster bombers. The photograph was taken on the present playing fields, with the station in the background. Many minor county cricket matches have been played here at Egloshayle – in 1986 Cornwall played Canada on the ground. Over the years, and at their best, Wadebridge have been a great force in East Cornwall cricket, having appeared in as many as ten finals between the years 1957 and 1973, winning the Cornish championship twice and sharing it once with Truro.

THIS EVOCATIVE photograph of a threshing machine at work is something of a mystery. Neither the author nor the publisher know the identities of the people in the picture or where this record of farming life in North Cornwall was taken.

33595A Tintagel, King Arthur's Castle.

◀

Sheep grazing among the ruins of Tintagel Castle.

◀

THE COVE at Tintagel. This is the heart of King Arthur country in Cornwall. Historians still wrangle – did Arthur reign in fact or fiction?

STEEP STEPS lead to Tintagel Castle – the Castle Hotel can be seen in the distance on the right. The steps are numerous amd precipitous, this great headland towers 270 feet above the sea.

THIS PHOTOGRAPH of flooding at Camelford Station in the 1940s underlines the fact that Camelford has some of the highest rainfall in Cornwall. There is no railway station at Camelford today. Visitors used this station on their visits to Tintagel and Boscastle and publisher Michael Williams recalls meeting guests at this station as recently as the 1960s.

CAMELFORD TOWN HALL: In 1884 the Corporation was abolished and the property of the Borough was vested in a newly created Camelford Town Trust. The Trust, now the Town Hall, was built in 1806 by the 6th Duke of Bedford, with a cupola containing a clock and two bells on a site previously occupied by the yarn market.

THE CLOCK TOWER at St Teath. 'The name is pronounced to rhyme with death', said Sir John Betjeman. 'It is a parish of slate ...' The White Hart, the building on the left was mentioned in a survey on 1806 but was largely rebuilt in its present form in 1884. The old kitchen, with its stone oven built into the stone fireplace, is now a snug bar. Back in the 1600s St Teath was the home of Anne Jefferies who performed miraculous cures – and people would come from miles away to see her.

ST TEATH village looking down the street towards the church. James Mildren in his Saints of the South West *gives us this profile: 'Patron of St Teath, and one of King Brychan's dozen daughters. Her sister, Adwen lived only a few miles distant. She is often referred to as St Tedda, and Nicholas Roscarrock says her feast day was observed on May 1, a day of much revelry on the Cornish Kalendars.'*

DELABOLE IS famous for its slate and quarry. In fact these gave birth and name to the North Cornwall village – and vital employment to generations of Cornishmen in the area. According to the Guinness Book of Records Delabole is the deepest man-made hole in Europe, more than 500 feet deep and over a mile in circumference. Delabole slate is a versatile durable material and in the form of roof slates, tombstones, gateposts, and boundary walls, has helped to shape the face of North Conrwall.

THESE CHILDREN at St Kew Highway look as if they may be about to set off for some special occasion. Certainly the photographer, so many years ago, must have had a reason for lining them up for his picture. Perhaps an older reader of the book may remember that special day.

▲ *Stormy day at The Rumps, Polzeath.*

▼ *A GENTLEMAN looks at cottages in Crackington Haven. A skilful piece of photography underlining the importance of bringing a figure into the picture.*

▲ *FORRABURY CHURCH, with its sturdy embattled tower, has a weather-beaten air. It was Forrabury that inspired Robert Stephen Hawker's dramatic poem* The Silent Tower of Bottreaux.

▼ *BOSCASTLE HAS an unusual harbour: a medieval breakwater, a long grey slipway and a huge dog-leg opening into the sea. This postcard was despatched from Cornwall on July 26, 1946.*

THE STEAM lifeboat, the Helen Peele *which took over at Padstow replacing earlier designs. The steam vessel was robust and reliable in the treacherous Cornish seas.*

THE COAST at Boscastle.

PADSTOW POINT – a typical North Cornish coastline in winter mood with its roaring seas and hidden rocks. Many a vessel has come to grief along these shores.

THE PADSTOW lifeboat, The Arab, *passing the Doom Bar. This is a clever piece of photography in that the finished picture is the result of three separate photographs being put together. But the fierce seas are real enough – and the courage of the men who manned crafts such as these is certainly not in question.*

AN OLD photograph of Padstow harbour, showing the location of the Strand Bookshop on the left. St Petroc chose this spot after his crossing from Wales some 1400 years ago, and his monastery here became an important religious centre. The Strand Bookshop acquired a kind of literary fame in 1986 when it was featured in a romantic novel entitled Impulsive Challenge *written by Margaret Mayo, and published by Mills and Boon.*

PADSTOW HARBOUR in 1906. This old Cornish port was the haunt of many great Westcountry sea dogs. Sir John Hawkins, for example, found shelter here in 1565 from the autumn gales when he returned from his quest for the North West Passage to China. Sir Walter Raleigh dropped anchor here, too.

PADSTOW HOBBY HORSE 1921 – though the true Cornish say 'Obby 'Oss. It is a fearsome animal wearing a fierce mask, more a heathen god than a living horse. Padstow's special place in British folklore occurs every May Day when crowds and age-old customs turn the narrow streets into a cauldron of music, singing and dancing.

A PEACEFUL Padstow picture from an old postcard. The author had strong family links with the North Cornish port. Her aunt provided lodgings for the Scottish girls who came to Padstow to smoke the fish, and her uncle was the town crier. He charged half a crown a time – unless it was for charity when he declined to take a fee.

THE MARKET SQUARE, Padstow. A horse waits patiently in the shafts for its driver and a little girl watches the photographer.

▲ *A GROUP OF men lay the railway track at Padstow in 1893. A journey from London took all day!*

▼ *THE MAJESTY of steam: a train leaves Padstow Station.*

▲

A BEAUTIFUL rural scene, captured by a photographer at St Merryn Office – date unknown. The district nurse beside her bicycle is reading – a letter perhaps. The lady in the door, with jar under her arm, is so natural that you realize many of these North Cornwall people were perfect 'models', as the painter Stanhope Forbes discovered on his painting excursions down at Newlyn. The small boy, jug in hand, is studying something quite intently but the little girl is on her way out of the picture.

▶

AN EVOCATIVE old photograph of Boscastle. This ancient hill has some Clovelly-like cottages. Boscastle, the village, the surrounding countryside and the dramatic coastline have all combined to make this area a powerful tourist magnet. Our picture, though, shows the face of quieter, more leisurely days.

Below: Snow-filled lanes near the main Camelford to Wadebridge road near St Teath.

Boscastle Village.

ST COLUMB Rectory which around the middle of the last century was considered, along with Bodmin and Truro, as a possible location for the Cathedral. The architect William White who was born in 1825 and died in 1900 has left this distinctive legacy in North Cornwall.

MOTHER IVEY'S BAY is a lovely stretch of Cornish coastline yet is rarely seen on a picture postcard. Here, however, is an old postcard showing the jagged cliffs and the lovely sweep of water. Not far away are the famous Cataclews Quarries which provided stone for many of our North Cornwall churches.

The Scrap Book

I sit and gaze through the pages
Of a scrap book old and rare,
That speaks of a land and a nation
And the past that they both share.

The old and crumbled cottages,
With greying, dusty cob,
Where once a man stood satisfied
Admiring a well done job.

A beautiful, sunny valley
Where the modern children play.
Once was a bed so soft, so green,
For a railway track to lay.

A majestic, powerful castle,
If history and legend are true,
Now it's a land well grazed, at rest
With sheep to guide you through.

Time's path has changed and danced
With a new direction and goal,
But the ancient wind is blowing
Speaking to the soul.

Mankind has come and rearranged
With his make-up box of steel,
But the sun is old and timeless,
So is the warmth I feel

For a land well loved, well worn
And a centuries' bountiful span,
Caught and kept in a scrap book
Cut by my Grandmother's hand.

KIRSTY GARDINER, born 1971, lives at Tregony. She has been writing poems and illustrated stories from the age of eight. Kirsty has a strong Christian faith and is proud of her long Cornish heritage. Here she contributes a poem especially commissioned for this book.

GRANNY AND GRANFER Lobb collect seaweed from Trebarwith Strand for fertilising their fields. Although there is development in the valley and in the cove itself, the beach and coastline are unchanged since those long-ago days. Scenes for a film called Malachi's Cove *were shot here in the 1970s. Based on Trollope's novel, it captured some wonderful Cornish images in his writing, and the film makers did precisely the same, especially in depicting some of the savage seas here.*

POLZEATH BEFORE the developers got to work at the turn of the century. The expansion of Polzeath into a popular holiday resort was inevitable. Its superb setting, that long sandy beach, the Atlantic surf and the cliffs all made it a natural. One travel writer twenty five years ago reflected 'Polzeath seems to grow more popular year by year. It is more modern and sophisticated in appearance than most Cornish coves.'

NEW POLZEATH – a very different sky line from that of the previous picture. New houses spread along the cliff – some perilously near the edge – and while the residents must enjoy superb views the scene for others has changed and the wildness of the cliffs has gone forever.

▲

THIS CHARMING photograph of a group of people and animals at St Endellion includes a little girl, then aged four. At the time of writing she is a lady in her 90s and still living in North Cornwall. Sir John Betjeman, who lived only a few miles down the coast described St Endellion as 'a windswept parish high on the Atlantic coast with much to show inland, and on its rugged slate coastline.' There is in fact a famous Festival of Music held in the Church every summer.

►

SIR JOHN Betjeman walking at St Enodoc. The most famous Poet Laureate knew and loved North Cornwall well. He died in May 1984 and is buried in St Enodoc churchyard set in the sand dunes near his North Cornish home.

PORT ISAAC beach before the breakwater was built. In the background on the right is the old school. Times were when Port Isaac was a busy fishing port with its own boatbuilding yards. The quay here was built in the reign of Henry VII, and the view up the coast to Tintagel Headland is one of the finest. Port Isaac somehow manages to retain an old world charm – the nooks and crannies intensifying the impression.

HARRIS'S TAXIS: Four taxis belonging to Mr Harris photographed at Polzeath beach in the late 1920s. Mr Harris was a Wadebridge man who owned a garage behind where the present post office is.

MODERN MACHINERY comes to Polzeath, but men and horses are still part of the scene even if the steamroller dominates.

THE WRECK of a French schooner in Port Quin, about 1906. Port Quin is a mixture of beauty and mystery in that the village died. One theory is that one night long ago all the men of the tiny sea port drowned in a storm and Port Quin became a ghost village. There are other possibilities. Did a combination of a bad fishing season and failure of local mines combine to send the men of the village elsewhere? Or did they all get cornered by the Press Gang and meet some cruel fate? Or was it simply that the fishing around the corner at Port Isaac looked a better proposition – and the villagers left?

CRABB
NTER & STATIONERS
BROS
Bodmin Fore

MENS
MUSIC
reet.

JAMAICA INN on Bodmin Moor as it looked 40 years ago. Thanks to Daphne de Maurier's novel Jamaica Inn it is now one of the most famous hostelries in all Britain. It was once a Temperance House – and has a haunted reputation. But nobody knows how or why it acquired the name Jamaica. In 1991 the A30 was reshaped and today Jamaica Inn occupies a safer but more isolated position, high above the new road.

◀ *BODMIN FORE Street with a postman in the foreground and two little girls in their turn-of-the-century dresses.*

AN EARLY railway engine in Bodmin.

FORE STREET, Bodmin in festive mood: the shops and cafe were owned by Mr & Mrs Thomas George who ran the business until their deaths – Mr George died in 1925 and his wife five years later. Today this is Julian Foye's furniture shop. The photograph was kindly lent by Mrs Mary George, niece of the original owners, who remembers having tea there as a child.

BODMIN GAOL was built in 1778. Prisoners were hanged here for such incredibly petty crimes as burglary, stealing a watch and setting fire to a corn rick – though of course others hanged for the crime of murder. The Prison was in fact 'the last place on earth' for more than 50 men and women. All the hangings except four were carried out in public, outside the gaol walls. Among those executed here were the Lightfoot brothers, James and William, who murdered Nevell Norway on his way home from Bodmin Market in February 1840. His grave is in Egloshayle churchyard and so many people wanted to see his murderers hang that a special railway excursion was run from Wadebridge to Bodmin.

AN OLD PICTURE postcard of Roche Rock with its hermitage perched on top – a solitary outcrop on the fringe of the high downs which lie between Bodmin and St Austell. In Cornish folklore it has a special place – though some think it was once a setting for pagan rites. When Christianity first came to Cornwall, introduced by Celtic saints from Ireland and Wales, a small oratory was built here. After the time of Tristan and Mark, late in the Middle Ages, a more elaborate hermitage was built, dedicated to the Archangel Michael, the saint of high places and the vanquisher of evil forces.

ST BREWARD Church is named after a warlike thirteenth century Bishop of Exeter who fought against the infidels in Palestine. The village was once known as Simon Ward – and Simon Ward was apparently the brewer to King Arthur's Court! So maybe King Arthur's Downs nearby are aptly named. In terms of location St Breward Church must surely be one of the highest, if not the highest church in the Diocese of Truro.

THE MANOR of Glynn in the Parish of Cardinham belonged for many generations to the ancient family of the name – from Domesday in fact, though not continuously occupied by the Glynns. In 1805 Mr E.J. Glynn starting building a new house at Glynn but before the interior was finished it was accidently destroyed by fire, a magnificent library perishing in the blaze. Mr Glynn was the last member of his family to live there. The walls were left fairly intact and Glynn was bought and restored by Sir Richard Hussey Vivian of Truro in 1841, he had been one of Wellington's generals at the Battle of Waterloo. More recently this late Georgian house has been owned by Dr Peter Mitchell, a Nobel Prize winner.

BOLVENTOR CHURCH is no longer in use. The register of this church reflected the hardness of life on Bodmin Moor in the mid 1800s. The novelist E.V. Thompson in Discovering Bodmin Moor *recalled: 'The first baptism is of Fanny, daughter of the toll-gate keeper at Palmers Bridge. The first marriage is of a tin-streamer and both he and his young bride scratched out an 'X' in place of a signature. But perhaps the burials reveal more than anything else the harsh environment of the moor. Most are babies whose frail consitutions could not withstand the damp and raw cold of a lonely moorland hut'.*

ST BENET'S ABBEY, Lanivet. There is a reference in Lake's Parochial History, *volume III: About a quarter of a mile to the south of the church stands S. Benets, once a religious house, but almost wholly unknown to history. "As to S. Benets" writes Dr Oliver, "asserted to have been a nunnery subordinate to some foreign monastery in Italy in France, or elsewhere (for various places have been named) it was nothing more than a chapel of special devotion, as is proved by a document, dated May 1535, in Bishop Veysey's register."'*

In this century, in the 1930s, St Benet's was rented to a Mr Middleton who opened the gardens to the public. There was a wishing well at the back, and one day a lorry driver stopped to make a wish because his son was missing. When the driver got home his son had returned.

MRS SINGER'S orchestra who made much music in North Cornwall and were Cornish dance band champions in the 1940s – winners of the accordion section. Those were the days and nights when the wireless – not television – reigned in our Cornish homes and a night out meant a visit to the local dance hall to enjoy music from a band like this.

ROAD TRAFFIC ACCIDENT involving a car and a cow in the early days of motoring. A policeman checks the animal – which appears very dead – and the other makes careful notes. There is no sign of the driver, a wheel lies in the hedge. One can only hope he emerged from the incident unscathed.

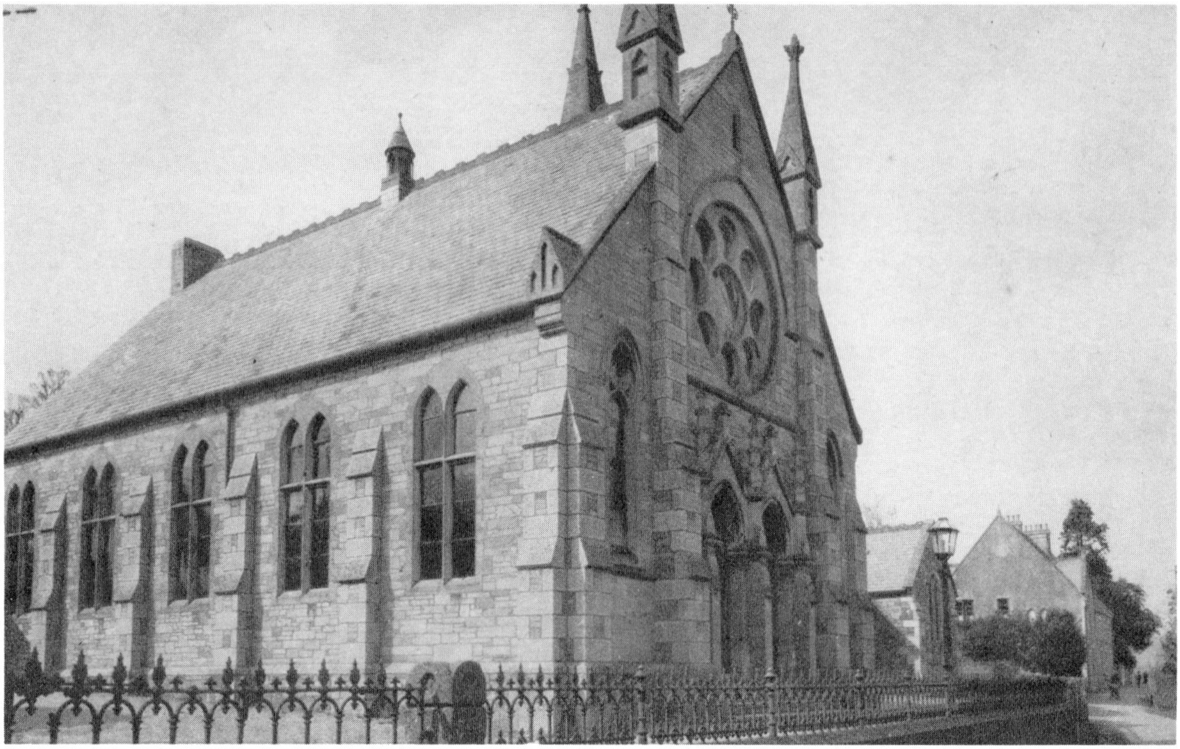

THE WESLEYAN CHURCH, Lostwithiel. The preacher John Wesley made many visits to Cornwall and the landscape is littered with chapels, reminders of Wesley's fiery message and his impact.

Wesley's physical achievements alone were enormous. He rode over 250,000 miles, sometimes covering 70 miles and delivering three sermons in the same day. He preached more than 45,000 sermons – and even here in Cornwall had to cope with hostile assemblies and the occasional riot.

ST MARY Magdalene Church, Launceston is not only one of the great sights of Launceston, but in the whole of North Cornwall. Consecrated in 1524, it is a remarkable building. Music in many varied and talented forms is found in our beautiful Cornish churches, and in the field of organs this church has something rather special. The organ here was presented to the Church by a member of the famous Morice family, then in residence at Werrington Park.

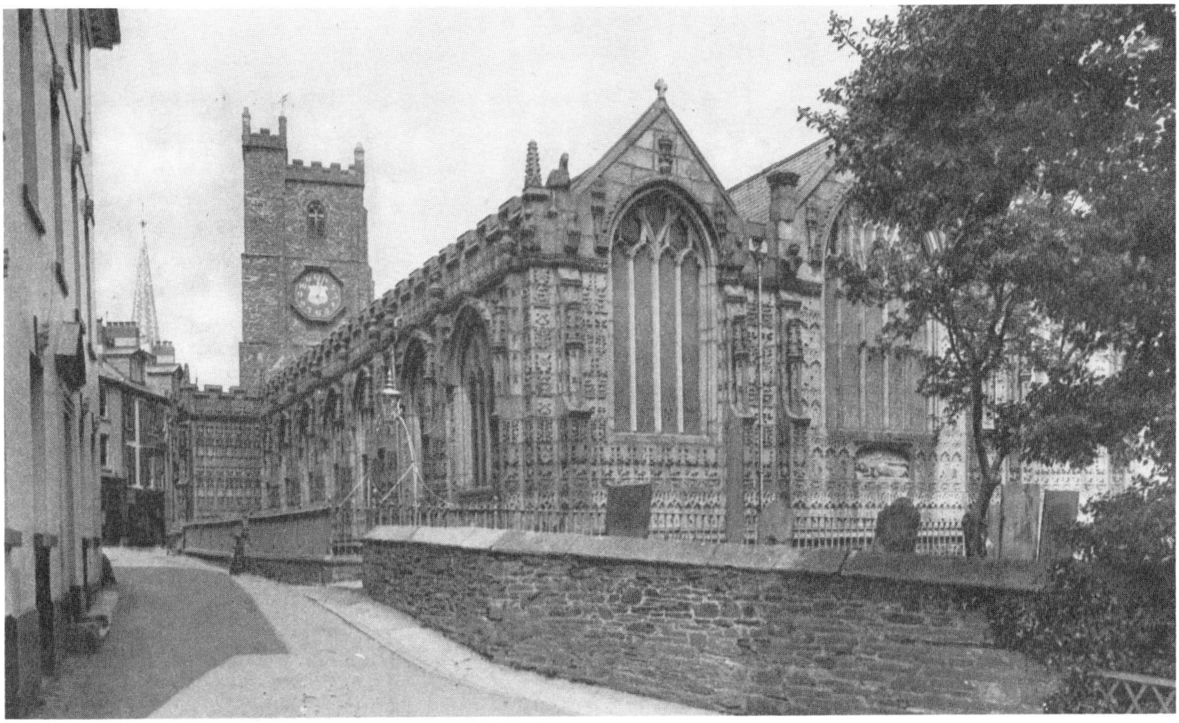

ST STEPHEN'S HILL, Launceston. This is a beautiful photograph by an unknown photographer. Did the lady simply emerge from one of the houses – or is she in the picture as a model? Either way, she is being observed by two young ladies by the street light. St Stephen's Hill is to the north of the town. No cars in this photograph, but today lorries and cars climb this hill in their thousands heading for Bude and Stratton and other places in the northern corner of Cornwall. Launceston is often called 'The Gateway to Cornwall' by virtue of its geography: just across the border from Devon.

THE BELLS about to be installed at St Thomas's Church, Launceston. Every fifty years the bells have to be rehung due to the wear through being rung, which makes the tone incorrect. Though not as ornate as St Mary's, St Thomas's Church has many interesting features, including a beautiful square font, probably brought from the Priory and fine pillars and arches.

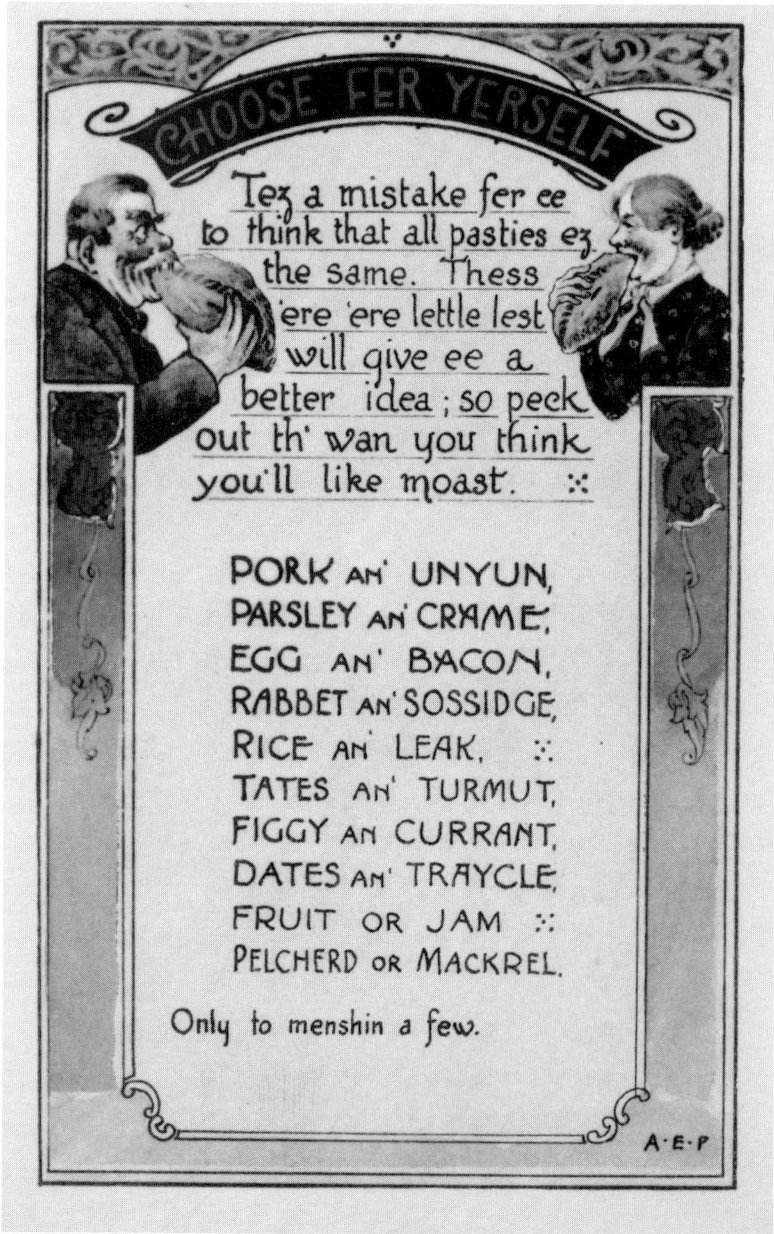

THE CORNISH PASTY can be a feast in itself – a moveable feast at that. Miners in particular valued the pasty because they could take their meal underground, but for some strange superstitious reason Cornish fishermen were loath to take a pasty to sea. In the mines there was a strange little tradition in the old days: a miner was supposed to leave a corner of his pasty for the 'knockers', as the evil spirits were called. It must have been a terrible temptation because many of us think the corner is the best bit!

Cornish Fishermen & Miners

PERHAPS THESE sturdy miners and fishermen were debating the merits of a pasty to go with the jug of ale or cider carried by the young fellow on the left. More likely the old miner seated on the rock had a good tale to tell at the end of his shift.

THE HARBOUR at Newquay – this picture postcard was presumably printed and published during the Hitler war, because on the other side of it is a quote from the Prime Minister: 'Let us strive without failing in faith or in duty.' The picture by an unknown photographer shows the little cove guarded by two very solid stone piers. Newquay has, of course, grown into an important tourist centre. Sir John Betjeman more than a quarter of a century ago wrote: 'It has vitality and vulgarity.'

DANCING ON THE beach at Newquay, perhaps between the wars. The town band is resplendent in its uniform, the chalets neatly lined up above the beach but the dancers are a bit scarce on the ground.

CORNISH WHIMSY – the folk traditions of Cornwall were swiftly turned to advantage by the locals cashing in on the influx of tourists. 'Piskies' mushroomed everywhere and here have even crept on to a postcard.

PEACEFUL WATERS of the River Camel. Perhaps the two small children in the boat are being taken out for a treat by mother and grandmother. Or is the boatman just ferrying them across? There is plenty of traffic on the river near the famous bridge at Wadebridge.

A LYRICAL photograph, from a picture postcard of the old Wadebridge and Bodmin railway – incredibly only 15 years after the Duke of Wellington's famous victory at Waterloo. Published by J.E. Davey of Wadebridge, this photographer clearly had an eye for a picture. Apart from the beautiful avenue of trees. there is a wonderful sense of journey.

THE FIRST train at Wadebridge. It travelled from Wadebridge to Bodmin, and passengers often got out to pick primroses or other wild flowers. They then rejoined the train while it was still moving as it only travelled at five miles per hour. A railwayman sat on the front of the engine throughout the entire journey ensuring the line was clear.

FOUR RAILWAY men pose for this picture at Wadebridge Station. Working for the railway in its smart uniform was a sought-after job. There was security – wouldn't the railways be there for ever? – and the pride of belonging to a valued and modern organisation. Railwaymen were a cut above the miners and farm labourers and could aspire to become a top-hatted stationmaster with unbelievable power.

WAITING FOR the train at the level crossing at Wadebridge. Time was when there was a foot bridge over this crossing, and the pedestrians could walk over the line.

THE LAST train at Wadebridge, photographed by the author in 1978. These lines were taken up two days after this photograph was taken. On the left is Levers Court Stores, where Leo's now stands. The author's second husband was a ganger working on this line, and picture was taken on the Saturday. By Monday the lines had been taken up.

LEAFY CORONATION Park.

TAKEN FROM the bottom of Gonvenna Hill, Wadebridge, this photograph shows Derry's Shoeing Forge, today a garage. Also shown is the Ship Inn.

WATERSIDE SCENES: Above at Sladesbridge, below, at Wadebridge.

EGLOSHAYLE CHURCH, Wadebridge.

THE CHURCH of St Breock was built in the thirteenth century. The fact that it has such a lengthy nave is probably because the Bishop held ordinations here. St Breock is the parish church of Wadebridge for the River Camel divides the parish of St Breock from that of Egloshayle.

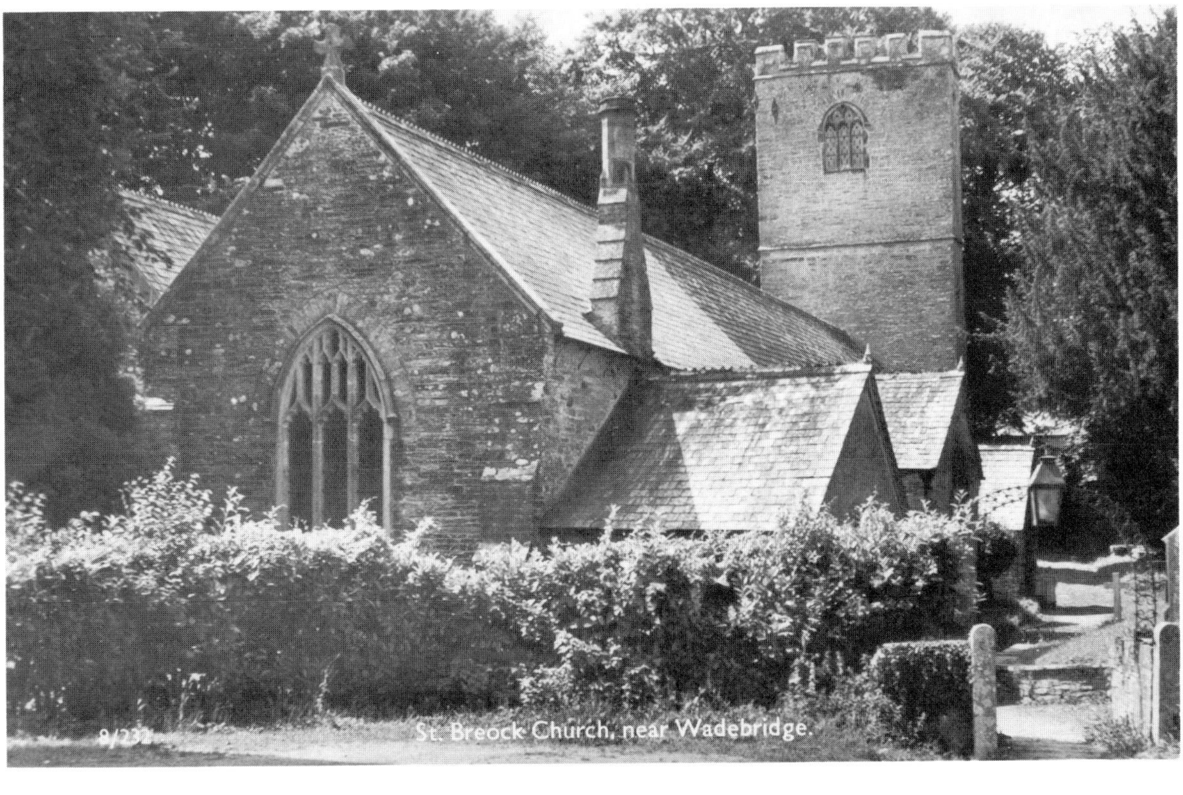

A WADEBRIDGE concert party: left to right back row: Mr Chapman, Mrs Harris, Mrs Weeks and Mr Job; front row: Mr Lander and Mr Latchem. Such concert parties were very popular and would give shows at village halls and schools, sometimes in private houses.

THIS GRANITE, from De Lank Quarry, was brought by train to the Quay at Wadebridge. It was cut, and then taken to be used on the Eddystone Lighthouse, transported by boat around Land's End, and up the other coast to Plymouth. The house in which the author lives is in Eddystone Terrace built by the men shown in this photograph.

ORGAN JOE – a popular figure with children, the organ grinder would tramp the towns and village of Cornwall turning the handle of his music machine wherever people gathered and were likely to throw a penny or two into his hat.

COLOURFUL CHARACTER – North Cornwall in the old days was full of character – and characters. Here is one such personality: Rosey Tucker who collected rabbit skins. As the caption to this old photograph shows, Rosey had earned himself the title 'celebrity'.

MISS DERRY standing in the doorway of her shop with its inscription 'Plumber and Bellhanger, Sanitary Engineer'.

MISS DERRY who owned a china shop that also sold plumbing and sanitary ware. Her shop is now Jago's in Molesworth Street, Wadebridge, and the doorway and steps are still there.

THE OPENING of Wadebridge Town Hall in the spring of 1888. It was then called the Molesworth Exchange. It was built of local stone with granite dressings. It is surmounted by a splendid eye-catching clock tower and over the entrance are the arms of the Molesworths of Pencarrow. The magnificent stained glass window was given by Viscount Clifden.

►

THE TOWN HALL at Wadebridge taken by Ray Bishop before it was restored. The clean appearance of the street is no illusion – it has just been snowing.

WAGGONER DELIVERING goods from Locketts warehouse. The picture was taken in the early years of the century and the driver is Mr Blank Irons.

MORE BOSSINEY BOOKS ...

AROUND & ABOUT THE SMUGGLERS' WAYS

by David Mudd

Working through almost forty different sources, including the records of H.M. Customs & Excise itself, David Mudd (who discovered in the course of his research that his great-grandfather was a Customs officer) has produced a book that is as heady and addictive as the spirits, the wines and the tobaccos that once followed fish, tin and copper as Cornwall's great industries. Several of the sketches and many of the photographs are by David's wife, Diana.

'... scrapes the romantic glitter from Cornwall's erstwhile illicit trade ... Meticulously researched and written in David Mudd's lively factual style it makes absorbing reading.' Alison Poole, Leader Group of Newspapers

AROUND NEWLYN, MOUSEHOLE & PAUL

by Douglas Williams

In a skilful combination of research and interviews – and a rich harvest of old photographs – Douglas Williams shows the powerful spirit that draws people back to this corner of West Cornwall has not been quenched.

MOUNT'S BAY

by Douglas Williams

In words and pictures Douglas Williams takes us from Land's End to Lizard Light, the most westerly and southerly point of Cornwall, enclosing a bay 'as majestic as any in Europe.'

DAPHNE DU MAURIER COUNTRY

by Martyn Shallcross

A special look at Cornwall in which the internationally-famous novelist set important stories.

'A treasure chest for those who love Cornwall and the du Maurier novels.'
Valerie Mitchell, The Packet Group of Newspapers

SUPERSTITION AND FOLKLORE

by Michael Williams

A survey of Westcountry Superstitions: interviews on the subject and some Cornish and Devon folklore.

'... the strictures that we all ignore at our peril. To help us to keep out of trouble, Mr Williams has prepared a comprehensive list.'
Frank Kempe, North Devon Journal-Herald

MY CORNWALL

A personal vision of Cornwall by eleven writers then living and working in the county: Daphne du Maurier, Ronald Duncan, James Turner, Angela du Maurier, Jack Clemo, Denys Val Baker, Colin Wilson, C.C. Vyvyan, Arthur Caddick, Michael Williams and Derek Tangye with reproductions of paintings by Margo Maeckelberghe.

'An ambitious collection of chapters.' The Times, London

AROUND & ABOUT THE FAL

by David Mudd

'David Mudd's book brings to life the many aspects of one of Cornwall's most loved rivers.'
Sarah Foot, Cornish Scene

SAINTS OF THE SOUTH WEST

by James Mildren

'This book, well illustrated with photos and sketches of buildings, monuments and the countryside associated with them, is a marvellous taster.'
Dr James Whetter, The Cornish Banner

GHOSTS OF CORNWALL

by Peter Underwood

Peter Underwood, President of the Ghost Club, journeys across haunted Cornwall. Photographs of haunted sites and drawings of ghostly characters all combine to prove that Cornwall is indeed a mystic land.

E.V. THOMPSON'S WESTCOUNTRY

A memorable journey: combination of colour and black and white photography from Bristol to Land's End.

'... the well-known novelist takes us on a memorable journey ... tells us of "the style and spirit of the region, its tone and tempo."'
Western Times and Gazette

WESTCOUNTRY HAUNTINGS

by Peter Underwood

'The Westcountry offers ... just about every kind of ghostly manifestation ...' writes Peter Underwood, President of the Ghost Club. '... a chilling look at hauntings from Bristol to Cornwall ... many of the accounts appear for the first time.'
David Henderson, The Cornish Guardian

THE CRUEL CORNISH SEA

by David Mudd, 65 photographs

David Mudd selects more than 30 Cornish shipwrecks, spanning 400 years, in his fascinating account of seas and a coastline that each year claim their toll of human lives.

'This is an important book.'
Lord St Levan, The Cornish Times

CASTLES OF CORNWALL

by Mary and Hal Price, 78 photographs and map.

St Catherine's Castle and Castle Dore both at Fowey, Restormel near Lostwithiel, St Mawes, Pendennis at Falmouth, St Michael's Mount, Tintagel, Launceston amd Trematon near Saltash. Mary and Hal Price on this tour of Cornwall explore these nine castles.

'... a lavishly illustrated narrative that is both historically sound and written in a compelling and vivid style that carries the reader along from one drama to the next.'
Pamela Leeds, The Western Evening Herald

We shall be pleased to send you our catalogue giving full details of our growing list of titles for Devon, Cornwall, Dorset, Somerset and Wiltshire as well as forthcoming publications. If you have difficulty in obtaining our titles, write direct to Bossiney Books, Land's End, St Teath, Bodmin, Cornwall.